Verso

Verso

Pattie McCarthy

Apogee Press
Berkeley · California
2004

Grateful acknowledgements to the editors of the following publications in which these poems (or excerpts from these poems) appeared:

26, eds. Avery Burns, Rusty Morrison, Joseph Noble, Elizabeth Robinson, Brian Strang; *American Letters & Commentary*, eds. Anna Rabinowitz & Matthea Harvey; *DC Poetry Anthology 2002* (dcpoetry.com), eds. Jules Boykoff, Kaia Sand, Tom Orange; *Free Verse*, ed. Jon Thompson; *ixnay magazine*, eds. Chris & Jenn McCreary; *Kiosk*, eds. Gordon Hadfield, Sasha Steensen, Kyle Schlesinger; *Pom^2*, eds. Allison Cobb, Jen Coleman, Ethan Fugate, Susan Landers; *P-QUEUE*, ed. Sarah Campbell; and *UrVox*, ed. Lee Ballantine.

alibi (that is : elsewhere) was published as a chapbook in the Duration Press e-books series (durationpress.com), ed. Jerrold Shiroma.

Cover Image: by an unknown FBI photographer (1960), courtesy of Joan McCarthy

Book Design: Philip Krayna Design, Berkeley, CA. www.pkdesign.com

©2004 by Pattie McCarthy.

ISBN 0-9744687-4-6. Library of Congress Catalog Card Number 2004105426.

Published by Apogee Press
Post Office Box 8177
Berkeley CA, 94707-8177
www.apogeepress.com

for Corey James,
Aidan James,
& Luke Joseph McCarthy

Contents

otherwise (an eke name) : 9
alibi (that is : elsewhere) : 27
piseogs : 51
sources : 67

This then, I thought, as I looked round me, is the representation of history. It requires a falsification of perspective. We, the survivors, see everything from above, see everything at once, and still we do not know how it was.
—W.G. Sebald, *The Rings of Saturn*

otherwise (an eke name)

does this heap mark the scene of a death or other disaster ? what was that disaster ? tell all you can find out about it. disorb, knock the thing from itself. unseen. she was busy with learning & became an adult in one piece. there is nothing I can do for your present relief. is there. not everyone's voice is the same weight. lineation of years & a year is an object or an ism in your pocket. a cure in time. the kiss was clumsy because this is not your native tongue. that's what happens when a nadder becomes an adder. I have about as much of that language as a moderately well-behaved dog needs to know. or less than. not more likely than not. emote dust. recidivist mendicant tendencies. disapproves of casual miscellany. & looks terribly proud of looking terribly thin. translating it from English into English— afraid we'll have to retroactively adjust the cause now that the effect is made obvious. they've provided a useful timeline so that we can watch the same mistakes made & made over & forgotten & marvelled over again. a timeline so that we can watch our own mouths moving. asked 'what hour is it' I offered my wrist. if only it would come to pass. she made with seaweed & her own feet the ground beneath them.

      old trope   thirty-one words
              seaweed—   I'm sorry I begot

winter proper   dispositive potato fog

    they drove out of the map's range
    they had to wait for new maps

                  "they murdered each other" / "of course   always"

part of me is charmed
this is my real mouth

how were people who trod on such places said to be affected ? any stories about people who were struck hungry at one of these places ? with seaweed she, her own feet— the sound of voices in stone buildings, high ceilings— voices speaking, not singing (which some buildings are made for). make a mark here (where things begin to look familiar). he made with little gestures the shapes of letters in the air. he insisted it was an endearment & the Polish for 'selfish.' Flanders was a country before it was a battle. if we linger, we'll be up to our lips in it. ITEM : underneath a field of rubble there must be something of interest or else there would be no sense in it. the name by which I know her has a different vowel-to-consonant ratio than the one with which she was born. there's documentation to prove all the consonants she's since forgotten. coyly, you've been leaving verbs around for me to find. the OE 'steorfan' meant simply to die before it took on the particular sense of to die by hunger. fingerling— starveling. my mind set asunder, my mouth turned awry. ITEM : there would be no sense in it— otherwise (or alias) it is merely evidential of itself. & we are kind to each other. it's a true story. we are kind in incremental gestures, codified gestures, to each other. it's a story told as though it is true.

they are intent on digging
they sold the ground out from under their feet

      there are postcards   this peculiar landscape   striped

          intertidal   rua   granite fingers
                                      send us boats or send us coffins stop

wrack equals weed
underneath a field of rubble
a timeline so that we

have there been cases where two or more children of a family had the same christian name ? how did this happen ? write down all such names, making a list of diminutives or pet-names : name-forms ending in -een (Jim-een, Pad-een), -ie or -y (Willie, Paddy, Oney, Norry), & so on. a more solid earth, granite edged— peaty acidic. despite intertidal episodes & bog pockets. put your foot down. cut a square foot to secret away, heavy. it is not merely the means of finding curiosities, archaic decorations. the imposition of hands, setting astray made straight. [there was a 'Frankie,' a cousin, who had a sibling that died. the parents were saddened of course, but they said 'at least it wasn't Frankie.' then Frankie died.] if she has sufficiently distinguished herself to be recorded by history : how will it spell her. I drank a lot of tea, didn't get hungry, & waited there for you. the ground apportioned in the most complicated manner— a medieval multiplication table based on factors of four. not that they didn't have word for it. I don't know enough about shapes, honestly. he says 'thing' as though Grimm's Law was a fiction. assume the word 'and' includes the word 'or,' & vice versa; the word 'any' includes the word 'all,' & vice versa. a mound of earth.

gort		gorta
versus		verso
gorta	v	gort

& when it is said that they sold the ground out from under themselves, it is meant quite literally— they cut it out & sent it off on donkeys, flat-bottomed boats, & so on. they had to wait for new maps. the basket's original use was for scooping potatoes in the air. one potato, two potato, three potato, wheretofore.

by what names were the various types of hillock, clump, hollow, swamp, vein & other features of bogs known ? how were the various kinds of mould, clay, ooze, & other matter called ? were there moving bogs in your locality ? "they murdered each other"; a cloud was a mound of earth. not that they didn't have a word for it — vowels of a language you thought was dead. with seaweed, with a mouth like a torn pocket, with an attraction to the land. a schist, a clod— everything I've read lately has a 'quag' in it, fair-gortha. [the empty lot with dead grass like Polish children's hair.] the ground beneath them proven. no plums in plum pudding, no meat in mincemeat. the OE 'drenchen' [to die by drowning] became the ME 'drench' [to get very wet]. deceptive appearances, &c. deceptive surfaces. a sour culture, moving borders & long winters. anecdotal evidence in a general summa containing all things. a timeline so that we can claim competent recognition of our own mouths moving. in the 9th c. they began (literally) cutting off their noses to spite their faces. & the barrenness of one landscape made the other bare. a place we refuse to name. someone takes a picture (the nostalgic quality of roofless houses ruined when I said something about evictions & taxes on covered out-buildings— I, a killjoy, have unintentionally squelched appetites).

a story told as though
it is true

aluminous— sun on water late   (send us boats)
jasny equals clear   bright   she told me blue
                                    she called her daughter blue

a name misspelled in the manifest
vowels of a language   sick to death

what expression is used to describe the act of adding a stone to the heap ? what is said while adding a stone to the heap ? where do people get the stones ? it could have been worse— it could have been a 'catastrophic success.' oxtail on a Sunday, the missing tongue of a bell. whores & horsethieves. intent on digging, that is what you will find there. ITEM : the edged weapon museum; the museum of unconditional surrender (verbatim). she hated lies like the following : he left because something put the sea between himself & the road; he left with grass in his mouth (&c.). she hated those sorts of stories told as though they were true. therefore, their leavings were wordless. nothing singular, nothing unusual. make a mark where you begin to look familiar, inter alia. mulch, rain— recidivist dread of optimists. still, we are kind. & planted birches so something might sound like him (she can't bear to hear his name spoken from an altar). therefore, we left early & wordless. the consonants (four, a single sound) were marbles— or burrs. speaking of, I went into the burdock after the dog & thought we would have to cut them out of mine, hers. not that there isn't a word for it. parentheses, the sea.

we eat well
with a healthy   skepticism
                  parentheses (the sea)

              "to live with potatoes   not to eat them
             but to live with them"

    a schist breaking down   bracken-infested
    land   a touch   the hand of a posthumous child

pickle it all   (one never knows)
the cartographer's nerves are wrecked

was it said that children who drew blood from one another in play should marry later? dirge, verso. envy & slavic melancholy— that we might dance on it. the borders are sour & served with cabbage. we begin with departure. a greener banality, a causal miscellany. we cannot determine where the line is. it is manmade (which is not exactly interchangeable with artificial, but here it is. artificial, that is). every dirge threatens to turn into a jig, every head threatens to turn on its spindle. were we to return in fifty perhaps they would still be there, playing. the curtain never falls, never terminates. I wished to be in circumstances requiring a telegram. the clusters of a language extruded through history— syllabified like little rocks. your native tongue returns spinning. women & children first. but first to what— I find no comfort in this particular indeterminacy. refresh your memory (a term of art). we have the documents to do so. where 'any' includes 'all,' any song is intentional (send us coffins stop). windows left open at night; birds in our life again. the real color of my mouth; facts not in evidence. it was cold & so I misspelled many simple things. there were roadside apparitions that summer— & dark & romantic soups [talking English, a stream of Magyar, Polish what]. my nostalgia is punitive.

& every dirge vice versa
"   it is always & everywhere the same, monotonous
          & desperate in its tedium, always

          the same song   "

& it never sounds to end   instead   the players
take the odd break from it   possibly only so that we
          the listeners

can rest   reel (a lively
round) performed by a couple in duple meter
whirl   spool   field   fiddle

what remedies were popularly recommended to prevent or counteract such wanderings (recital of special prayer, turning of coat inside-out, dust thrown into eye of bemused person) ? having a surface that yields. jointed for desire, fingers flex, curl. digging with a sense of purpose. a true story, a streak of melancholy running down her neck, with seaweed & her own feet she re-made beneath her the ground — but she would not have recognized herself as such. the most popular proposed location of purgatory was in Lough Derg. borders, currents. current borders. in hollow unison, gallows-eyed, our mouths move. high ceilings, a stone building designed with an eye toward the history of its own decay. unearthed. ITEM : "the rubble of recognition." a nonce-word, perhaps— for the name's sake [out of regard for one's name, that is]. a timeline marking pejoration (whore) v. amelioration (queynt). in bed, I think of something I must read & get up to find the book (Kapuściński's *Imperium*). in it, serving as a bookmark, a Czechoslovakian 20 korun note— the original words partly obscured by a glued-on patch reading Slovenska Republika.

he could talk the noose off
his neck & so   can I

"nostalgia   is essentially history without guilt"

for 6 bells   720 strikes ring all possible changes
each arrangement particular   signalling danger weather birth war hours

    the peculiar combination of sounds
    employed as the individual designation

the name by which I know her

have many generations of the same line been alive at the same time ? did the number ever reach five or six ("rise, daughter, and go to your daughter, for your daughter's daughter has given birth to a daughter") ? from the church tower, the song cuts off abruptly mid-phrase. everyday at the same time. in the manifest, he listed as his nationality one that no longer existed. of obscure etymology, 'girl' was of flexible gender until the 16th c. they had to wait for new maps. anecdotal evidence. someone who has lost the habit of conversation. she requested her birth certificate & received a letter two weeks later— no such person. (she'd inadvertently dropped a vowel into a consonant cluster.) despite appearances— 'in pursuit of the unpronounceable'— all spelling is consistent & phonetic. yielding surface. the history section overrun by memoirs. [suggestions to cottagers : commence with YOUR DISEASED POTATOES, by washing them well, then peel or scrape off the skins, carefully cutting out such parts as are discoloured.] decimate originally referred to killing every tenth person. my people are flatterers & nincompoops. a timeline upon which borders are redrawn & disappear at regular intervals. I read it somewhere : we say, 'they said.' a voice, then voices. noise, distortion forms a ground, sea-girt. random rubble construction— dry fences, sods & hedges, wattles or wire. I envy them their memory.

the upper bright air   a kind gesture   (either / or)
a stile without stones loose

    the name by which I know
    her   a story told
       as though it is true   "they murdered
                                                        each   other"
                it begins with departure

alibi (that is : elsewhere)

One of a million medieval bright ideas was that
the air was made of invisible wings.
— Laird Hunt, *The Paris Stories*

nonesuch auguries, egads.
we will have none of that.
saying again this place is
this, only moreso.
here the air
rises from beneath it
seems & is heavy salty—
whereas there the air is sharp,
takes corners, comes around
corners sharply.
it hasn't rained for fourteen days. the birds
have thwarted me & eaten the verbena seeds.
I smell like a girl & tire of profundity.

if it is to be a nor'easter it should at least snow. how do you spell 'forego' ? In 1878 Thackeray wrote : women are not so easily cured by the alibi treatment. concerning the black death, 'hippocratic katastasis' is understood to mean the way the air stood still with malice aforethought. if the air does not move, no one will be well. I believe I managed to arrive here by the invisible string that attaches my car to traffic, to the car immediately in front of mine. See Chaucer (*Troylus*) : I have eke foundyn by astronomye, By sort, and by augury eke truly. See Shakespeare (*Hamlet*) : Not a whit, we defy augury. There is special providence &c. if it be not now, &c. I know there is something to wheeling flocks, there is something to droughts & good earth. I will teach you how to chart the longitude & latitude of approaching hurricanes where we go to take the air— they say there is something in the air, negative ions : they ease the mind. they produce good dreams & heavy sleep. *ion* is from the neuter present participle of "to go."

dear _____,
since I left your city, I've grown clumsy
& have bruises under several fingernails—
smoke too much & wake up early
while the sun is still on the porch
which is a portico because wishing makes it so.
there is no air there. though I felt
comfortable when I'd wake up from there.
for a moment I thought in Flushing
last week in the morning & everyone
was much relieved. I continue to hear
my house sleep & when I hear it is no longer
sleeping I have words with the yarrow.

it is the property of air to be still
it is the property of air to move when it sees fit
the highest degree of Swooning
suspended animation
or apparent death by Drowning
the continued pulse with discontinued respiratory action
it indicates a curious infelicity of etymology
it was never either/or
it was explicit in its choicelessness
to inhale takes approximately two seconds
to exhale takes three
& when we've asked all we can ask of cigarettes & coffee
commence with the peripheral silver fish—

there one is afraid of that
which is invisible whereas
here one fears that which is seen.
with maps, one could endeavor to prove
one's self alibi.
no one leaves here ever if
only there was another.
it's not safe sometimes to meddle with walls.
the fall of Jane Scrope's sparrow.
if by making certain
conditions of the air— well, that's how they took
the poison in those days.

nicotine, rain, curry— you see, all yellow things
one expects to pine for. so watched a Belfast
movie that began sadly & ended sadly— neither
more sadly nor less sadly. rather, exact. & started
a letter : since I left your city.
we force the clock contrary to its hour :
  face east, the weather being clear,
  watch for birds, noting from whence they
  came, & in what sort they wag their wings, &c.
having given my mouth over to your inflections, that glamour
descends from grammar; having masterfully passed over nine
burning ploughshares, you propose to address me infanta;
morning, like a dog in a manger.

placebo— I allow
it's fatal to kill swallows.
a weather, of another kind I say :
cup of tea, cup of tea, cup of tea ?
he smites me. smitten, again I am
all the words I wear
indicating that this is so only
moreso. smitten—
& taken to wearing more metals
(look this up, what is augured there)
& spent the morning entire
explaining absinthe & semi-colons.
an effort to be sensible, to alter the material of air with mere pronunciation.

this is the miraculousness of caulk. the difference between a physic & physics. unstable quantitativeness. a gin & tonic with lime & quinine— I've seen you play the saint with your bitten fingernails, your sermon-crooked mouth, your iodized preservative. dear, since I left your city I bruise easily & sleep too much. butterfly bushes & the flutter cross the Atlantic, your lessons in chaos. such a day may require six hours of wittiness, forgoing responsibility for long walks, a comedy of manners, or a commentary on social errors. I am tidy & grateful & as earnest as all the backyards in Philadelphia. made a sheep from wax, a few parallel lines there scratched. happy birthday, Judas Iscariot.

the legal definition of *obligation*—
heir to your father's enemies. perhaps I am
curious for this place.
elsewhere is still
somewhere— but perhaps not
where the compass is— your
compass has fallen to earth & so.
a bird killed in the yard— feathers (white,
unusual) hither & thither.
evidence of a struggle. questions of proof & ethics.

laziness gave us *ampersand* & I am happier for it.
were we to wake very early to observe
staccato in the music of spheres or a prowler.
were we to discover therein the lack— all
the indignity, advances, & indifference one
must muster. you start
the day at odd angles & predestination
selects the coffeemugs. more spontaneous & less
superstitious, please. if not lazy, then a slur— in several
senses. a great unending existential schwa.

she used to find beautiful its angle in air.
she used to find beautiful
the juxtaposition of natural & manmade
things in air. she used to envy
its underbelly & imagined
destinations over the expressway. certainly
there's an accurate phrase for this in a language
I don't speak well. I'm prepared to forfeit
my self-righteousness in escrow at this time.
& (something) in the air— (something) uttered
or not, renunciation even.

quadrillion is a real word
& they all alight somewhere like so many
devices in heraldic lists—
although we only see
them wheel (gigantic) alongside the turnpike.
the bulk of it in air. what is augured
chaotic there. when I see you
next we will be strangers.
decisions are made in motion— a body
at rest decisionless. while there might be a phrase
that effectively describes it, merely arrive at a number.
she's a widow in her marrow. this is how
a person becomes debris.

given birds & the element through which
they have the privilege to move. a clarity
known as keening, out of earth
a body is. the tiny shapes in our mouths
don't match what we hear. since
leaving, I'm the occasional
victim of my own felicity & calculated ennui.
thus far, a gloveless & scarfless winter— here
one grows attached to things; or
bliss & boredom— that unholy alliance & certain
variability in the air. & remain (dear
sir, respectfully) aesthetically impatient.

the mud month— this is a leisurely & plural experience.
this is a serious financial gesture :
      a silent consideration of the disposition
      & movement of some thing.
a lit cigarette will lend the anecdote
a certain gravitas. our eye
follows the invisible line left behind.
our eye reads the line; or (rather)
the confusion of lines left by a fistful of iron
nails thrown to disperse things malevolent & airy.

the name by which she entered
history is not how she would have referred to herself.
cras, cras— the crow's
call understood as optimism— tomorrow.
tomorrow, all our accumulated throbbings
may be exhausted. melancholic & atlantic
as opposed to sanguine & pacific—
I have the honor to be &c.,
at its edges, the continent
appears to become a solid in the space
between sounds & the curious
darkness between birds. from a distance
one may become convinced of this—

the city in an airless moment— to speak without breathing. : a bridge is a public street crossing a body of water. bodies of water, being traversable, were weak points & medieval cities, as we have seen, were frequently walled off against them. if from my window I could see a bridge, a parliament of fowls. *I would imagine that the world was held together by the courses they flew.* I would argue that semantic differences are among the most important things. burdon : a note of long duration. endura : a foolish monument to starvation. simply not enough blood gets to my fingers. though they are, in fact, solid. a thing cannot be proof of itself; I cannot; you cannot. I could see a bridge.

air, dear [your name here]—
to see, to speak, to leave
the city choking & etched
inside my eyes. ex humus
corpus est : a stone for useful
objects, the materials of minimalist-
boy-sculpture. you should not
believe me. vernacular only
means not Latin but how else are we to talk
about plants, about practicality.
a manmade object, I
turn lights on & off, speak,
am spoken to, reply, dress, undress— yes,
I undress manmade & otherwise
engage with objects external
to myself. a gesture of location.

heavy things shift in flight. another
bird in the interim, an intermezzo circus.
knots in the air, unco lair. & history. I take these losses
personally, I admit. it is unseasonably
chilly & he effortlessly exchanges war for postwar
correspondent. we make these
preemptive & arrogant movements. vaulting is not too
ambitious a subject for summer travel, however—
the story goes like this & has too many commas.
the story was told to me as follows & will be on the final.
we eat beyond our means & recognize
the timeline as an absurd artifact. here, have a year.
a place where you resemble yourself, where they
resemble themselves. here my research
is far from complete & my reading insufficient.

we were there. & then
we came here. *queens under cabbages*—
a beach of little teeth, bleak horse.
under a word for not-rain in a language
we cannot call with any
honesty my grandmother's. speaking metaphorically
we can make this nostalgic
& nonsensical gesture, however.
what kind of thing is that to say ?
is that to say, that is. yes—
as though the phrase was itself
a soteltie & hence : a thing made
useless but pretty. baked in a pie.

if you turn left
here it is the end of earth— a more
solid earth you put your foot
down with a satisfying sound.
a scraggy field separated by another
scraggy field with over a thousand
given names— small, crooked, oddly
sequenced, loosely interpreted
rectangles. & inside those rectangles, shapes of a domestic
sort, the shape of gravity— roofless
things, their gables sharp. lapsing into the fantastic
or romantic a failure thus exhibited, the thin mimicry of it. taller, walls
crossed without knocking stones loose
                        this monu
                        mnt erectd
                        by his wyf

not the violent, disinterested property of air; nor one of the various categories of possible devastation; not sighing back at birds; not stitching clothes while in them; not that they don't have a gift for gentle, greatly understated euphemisms; not more likely than not; not territorial divisions; nor the space above those walls; it is not the particular twitch of every inch; not a relict, derelict house; nor a relict in a derelict house; it is not a catalogue of wind gusts & storm surges; not a chart that might predict something; not something about systems; not the confidence to say 'if it doesn't rain here, it will elsewhere' (however confident we may feel about that); not ankle-clutching vetch; not that vetch doesn't invite suspicion; not that cake wouldn't be nice; not that they didn't have a word for it during plague; not that they didn't have a word for it during famine either; not the roads & circles & not-quite roads that got us here; not this progress necessarily reversed; it is not asking : *should we have stayed at home & thought of here*; nor an accurate word between us in answer; not that I'm not amazed to find that there is something & not nothing; nor explaining a preference for land excerpted down to crag

it is our duty to doubt
we are obligated to a certain skepticism
we still say the air
is better here. we take overly dramatic
deep breaths as proof. the air here
: vegetable in quality & bigger. at night
it is darker & resists
suspicion in its very healthful spookiness.
I have no will to disprove this.
the air is autumnal, sheeogy & we've become
familiar & snobbish enough to profess to only
loving the place in winter, in inclement greyest weather.
it consoles us with the fiction that there might
be something still unknown here.

the faded marks, a revenant of an arch
which once led to an anchoress' cell—
a wall there now, but outside
the wall in the grass a cracked
long stone where here she lived & died.
where we are currently
wintering, there is no excess of granite.
the effects of wind
& rain & centuries (*of filthy weather*) of devoted
or merely curious hands on the carved beakheads—
or the finger labyrinth set in the wall.
also a recessed slotted box— it says 50p.

piseogs

Pishogue : (piʃoa'g) *Irish*. Also pishrogue, pishtrogue. [a. Ir. *píseog, písreog*. witchcraft: — M Ir. *písoc*.] sorcery, witchcraft; a spell, incantation, charm. 1841 S.C. Hall *Ireland* II 269 : Now a pishogue is a wise saw, a rural incantation, a charm, a sign, a cabalistic word, a something mysterious signifying a great deal in a little. 1854 T.C. Croker *Fairy Leg. & Trad. S. Irel.* (1879) 74 : He had no right to be bringing his auld Irish pishogues to Rome. 1859 P. Kennedy *Evenings Druffrey* xxvii, 3.7 : He threw pishrogues on our eyes. 1895 Barlow *Lisconnel* viii, 166 : Wrought through the agency of 'some quare ould pishtrogues'. 1901 M.J.F. McCarthy *Five Yrs. in Irel.* xiv. (ed. 5) 155 : The talk turned upon 'pishogues', or witchcraft & charms.
— *The Oxford English Dictionary*

A man named Michael Cleary in a state of almost incredible grievance, superstition and savagery, with circumstances of great cruelty burnt his wife to death on a kitchen grate under the belief that he was exorcising an evil sprit. In this extraordinary proceeding he was— more extraordinarily— assisted by several others including the murdered woman's father. I feel the incident is indicative of a vast amount of ignorance and superstition existent still among some of the Irish Peasantry.
—District Inspector Crime Special Pierris B. Pattison, 5 April 1895

there isn't enough blood in my veins to write my name.

she went with eggs & past the rath, took
like a trembling. great actual bodily harm.
forspoken, overlooked : I am going now. eschewed
the doctor's medicine & submitted her to some

fairy quackery. they say she was 'drawn away.'
blasted.
head in a sack, a gold earring in the left ear, & a pair of black stockings.
poc sídhe a pox
upon tomorrow
the walls of our house will be red.

I have stood in the door & I have heard lovely music.

Q.
what happened next ?
A.
she lit up like a blaze.

things they hate : iron, fire, salt, black-handled knives.

> when Lady Fanshawe saw a ghost in Ireland c. 1650, she & her husband stayed up all night debating why such apparitions were much more common there than in England; by morning they alighted on the cause : it lay in the greater superstition of the Irish.

were the curative herbs cast out along with them ? details.   purple foxglove— that is lus mór   lus na mban sídhe   originally folksglove   in Anglo-Saxon foxes glofa. going with the 'hair-of-the-dog' theory, will cure a fairy-struck child. other synonyms : witches' gloves   fairy's gloves   gloves of our lady   bloody fingers   fairy thimbles often found in the crevices of granitewalls, by roadsides, around rabbit-holes; children's pasttime of trapping bees in its flowers; recommended for those 'who have fallen from high places' & as a cardiac stimulant— that is, digitalis. in large doses, one may see everything as blue. (foxglove does not appear in Shakespeare.)   st. johnswort— the chief of the protective herbs. found in sunny pastures & should be gathered the morning of st. johnseve, since that night one must watch from the church porch for the specters of all who will die that year. harvest with care & crossings. protects the wearer against fairy blight & witchcraft [verbena has the same virtue, that is, vervain — sometimes also ferfaen]. that is, also herb of grace & herbus veneris (see aphrodisiacs). include it in your lustral water. bruised & worn around the neck to allay headaches, used as a febrifuge in autumn. Albertus Magnus recommends it against the pox & says it makes for good breath.   henbane— a poison : a remedy for warts, also gafann   hog's-bean   jupiters-bean   spurge   or the Anglo-Saxon henbell. waste sandy places, on rubbish heaps & near old buildings, particularly on chalky ground & near the sea. henbane may have killed Hamlet's father. however, one should note that in *Lyte's Herbal* (1578) it is recommended as a paste for earaches. perhaps it has been confused with the 'sleepy tree,' hebenus. a hallucinogenic : a poison : the leaves & roots if eaten cause maniacal delirium, or worse— cause an unquiet sleep which continues long & deadly.   & new milk— Kramer & Sprenger warned people not to give or lend butter, milk, or cheese to a begging witch. fire clings to fire   — like & unlike— & they say fire
comes from center.

wash your pails & cleanse your dairies; sluts are loathsome to the fairies.

such charges were often disguises for other social transgressions. there was a Singer foot-pedal sewing machine in her bedroom.

there, in the garden, the burial of my sillyhow.

      medle so mervelous (we are
          a marvelous mixture)

the night she died she wore a red petticoat, a striped petticoat, gray or green stays, a flannel dress & cashmere jacket (both navy-blue), a white knitted shawl, black stockings, black boots, & an 'ordinary' calico chemise. her ears were pierced.
the day he was arrested, her husband found the other earring in the ashpile.

    jabbin a babbin a baby's knee   holesum polesum sacra tea
potato rose single toes   out goes she

nervous excitement, bronchitis, middling. postmortem the lungs
were 'slightly congested.' the stomach appeared healthy, its contents not examined.

egg money in a coffee-canister under the bed.   'gentle' places
ringfort   sián   rath   rusheen   lios   fort   forth   cashel   cathair
the awkwardness of language in the area between the intimate & the scientific. maps show roads that detour in sudden half-circles. Bridget Cleary's dog pined for her.
a medal hung from a wide red ribbon, other talismans.

agatha's-letters— inscribed on tiles, bells, amulets— against fire.

since I was born in daylight my mother said I'd never see anything worse than myself. however, it was the morning of the last day of spring, so with the solstice I might get something yet. my grandmother from Cobh would not tolerate sheeogy talk— she went to college to study piano (Bowling Green, 1919). nevertheless, she said that since I was born on a Sunday there would be no cure in me.

if found four
leafed, one can
see through all
glamour   [& understand
what dogs say to one another]

      spots which differed in color or texture from the surrounding areas; spots where unusual sounds were heard or strange things were seen at night; lonely places; rock interfered with, cows die; funeral seen coming from rock at night; man who cut a stick in such a place has his mouth twisted; girl who is tripped in a certain house has her mouth turned awry; people are stricken with sudden loneliness or hunger, or lose their sense of direction in certain places.

Are you a witch or
      are you a fairy?
Or are you the wife of Michael Cleary?

something is just strange about a white horse.   one soot smudge on her forehead.

abduction as a convenient metaphor for : adultery, childlessness, various
bad behaviors. abduction as rationalization of infanticide.

recited with purpose, even when
mumbled, whispered, fast, incomprehensible,
untranslatable, the mere
repetition of formulae in a foreign
language, say so many paternosters, so many aves, say
them in uneven numbers.

Yeats never learned Irish—
yet claimed it not possible to speak an abstract thought in it.

    tigath tigath tigath calicet aclu cluel sedes adclocles acre earcre arnem nonabiuth
    ær ærnem nithren arcum cunath arcum arctua fligara uflen
    binchi cutern nicuparam raf afth egal uflen arta arta arta trauncula trauncula

        [she was the color of the wall]

take care not to clean up spilled milk—
& leave a few cold new potatoes outside.
a woman with butter in her mouth cannot be 'taken.'

Irish witchcraft statutes were based on English law— & despite popular belief
that witches were burnt, death by hanging was the British usual. unless 'petty treason'
had occurred (e.g. when a woman killed her husband or a servant his master). in practice,

> however, the Irish preferred burning : the first being Dame Alice Kyteler's maid, Petronilla de Meath, Kilkenny 1324. Dame Alice herself fled the country

(to England, oddly enough).

if one quart of cream should bring one pound of butter
but never does, where does the rest of it go ?
she was not herself. she was suspiciously
not herself. she crouched by the fire,

melancholy & cranky. 'she is not my wife. she is too fine to be my wife.' more on foxglove : if the wind changes directions while cutting it, you'll lose your mind. even better than that is saving & drying what's in the craw of a cock killed on st. martinseve. concerning garblus (that is, dandelion), if taken for illness related to fairies, if it doesn't cure it will kill straight away.

literate, relatively well-off, childless.

> had they hair, teeth, eyes, ears, blood ? could they talk or hear or see ? what language ? make a list.

Michael Cleary called for the doctor several times & also the priest— he tendered the viaticum. on the seventh day, he turned to other methods.
    they say priests that take some drink have courage enough to do cures, regardless of how often they speak officially against it. but whenever a priest reads over someone, something is lost (e.g. a calf, the priest's mind, &c.).

he put something in my mouth to save me.

this morning my dog was fighting a shadow.

Q.
how was a person to get out through the windows without breaking them ?
A.
while not a witchcraft expert, I imagine one could get out by opening the window.

this might be an opportune moment to consider the role of suggestion in healing :
    the chronic headaches of Anne, Viscountess of Conway, c. 1666, proved
    too much for the healing strokes of Valentine Greatrakes, the most
    famous Irish occult healer of the 17th c. still, he found
    success with scrofula & the ague before failing to demonstrate
    before Charles II, after which he was metaphorically whipped back to Ireland.

to move 'beyond
nine' is outside
reason. days as spatial
       as well as temporal.

                                            the man
                                            had killed
                                            the thing

three headlines from *United Ireland*, 13 April 1895 : The Tipperary Wife Burning, Boycotting Prosecution at Drogheda, & The Oscar Wilde Scandal. the verb 'boycott' comes to us from Charles C. Boycott, of Co. Mayo, who was ignored with great success by his tenants when he refused to lower rents. the press preferred to refer to Bridget

Cleary as a suspected 'witch' & not a suspected 'changeling' (since fairies are ambiguous
&— to an audience unfamiliar— harmless). changelings are children, readers would
think. ringforts are quaint, like daisy-chains.
a 'witch,' however, sells papers & is associated with death by fire.
the word 'fairy' as an epithet for a homosexual man didn't appear in print until 1896.

elf-shot. elf-lock.   [she took a lot of killing]

the wearing of words.

her trial lasted nine days (without a single attempt to escape). after nine,
there would have been nothing anyone could do.

the bane of cross & clever women.

the virtue of iron as a prophylactic
against enchantment.   everyone knows, however,
that there are seven herbs that nothing natural or supernatural can injure; they are
 : st.johnswort   vervain   speedwell   eyebright   mallow   yarrow   selfhelp :
best gathered at noon on a bright day near the full moon.

making a fairy of me now, & an emergency. he was truly vexed. he thought to burn me
three months ago.
the seventh brother of the seventh sister or the seventh sister of the seventh brother, or
something like that. that's what they brought, the seven cure from a woman in Fethard.
& gone about the house making piseogs.

                'I have herbs that there is nine cures in;
it will be very hard to make her take this.' new milk, or the first milk
given by a cow after calving, is known as beestings or nús.

when boiling it up, a drop of sour cream will crack it.
nine were [blank]
node's sisters, then [turned] the nine to viii, & the viii to vii, & the vii to vi, & the vi
to v, & the v to iiii, & the iiii to iii, & the iii to ii, & the ii to i, & the one to none.

the repetition of st. bridgets-Oes for fifteen days to divine the date of one's own death.

whether indeed on the low road she would meet the suicidal eggman from Ballypatrick.

    & the nine adders
    all weeds must now   give way to herbs
    the seas split apart,   all salt water,
    when I this poison   blow from you.

Monday & Tuesday are good days for pulling herbs— but a Sunday cure is no cure.

there should be metal in the bucket. attractive. her father forced open her mouth,
her uncle gripped her ears to hold her head down, one cousin held down her right arm,
his brother held down her left, & their youngest brother lay across her legs. it was bitter
& it took six men to make her take it & they held her mouth shut to prevent
it from coming back. iron & fire, black-handled knives. & asked in the name of god
whether she was who she was & she said twice
what they wanted to hear but refused the third.

then began the winding of Bridget Cleary. this requires at least two men.
he threw piss on her at intervals of twenty minutes.   the fireplace was cleared.
don't make a herring of me.

      the night I fell asleep there was   the night I fell asleep in the grass.

Dublin Evening Mail, 25 March 1895 : Civilization & humanity are much more precious, whether at Ballyvadlea or elsewhere, than the privilege of self-government, & we must not be made the sport of ignorant & superstitious cruelty. It is a lying claptrap that says 'Force is no remedy.'   Force is sometimes the only remedy for an evil.

next morning if you had gone
out you would have been up to the top of your boots in blood & hair—

or it could be these seven : ground-ivy vervain eyebright groundsel foxglove bark of elder-tree young shoots of hawthorn : mixed together in nine balls & afterwards boiled in bogwater with a piece of money & an elf-stone (found near a rath, lifted up). on my fingers metal sigils— a leftover belief in the efficacy of wearing words.

in order to fit
Bridget Cleary into her fireplace, she was curled into fetal position.

'her head was to the left of the grate, & her right hip rested on it; her legs were partly projecting out.' she did not scream. if the right questions are not answered by midnight, she might never come home again.   I am, Da.
a ritual healing completed three times. about midnight, tea was finally made. he put something in to save me. scraped off the roof of her mouth, rubbed into the blanket.

    malific if broken by the hand.   automatic gestures. a suspect shilling.
the compliment as curse.
    she will
    get her
    death this
    way :

never asked for milk without paying for it. & dressed
herself in her best— there was no use saying any more. I have eaten no bite
nor sipped no drink of theirs but cold mashed potatoes on my father's dresser

The Nineteenth Century, vol. 37 (June 1895) : That such superstitions should still be believed in a Christian country, & by men who by religion are Christians, is appalling enough; but the remedy for such a state of things is not to be found in the hangman's noose, nor yet, perhaps, in the convict prison, & one cannot but feel that it would be in the spirit of that wise & merciful law which ordains that boys under a certain age may not be hanged for capital offences to spare these men, even if they are condemned; for children they are if, as can, I think, be proved, they acted under the influence of such superstitious fears, as surely the savage who fears his own shadow is a child.

tipper-ipper-apper on your shoulder
tipper-ipper-apper on your shoulder
tipper-ipper-apper on your shoulder
I am your master

    was it considered wrong to say jokingly 'they're coming for me' when one heard
    an unusual voice ?

if neglected, fairies may wash their children in your beer.

Q.
don't you know it is with an old witch I am sleeping?
A.
you are sleeping with my daughter.

her second burial was held at night by lantern light with only policemen to attend her, beside the wall & her mother unmarked. she was given no wake, no service, a boycott. the coffin did not touch the consecrated surface earth.

letters on or near the skin, the better to get into the bloodstream.
      a needle under
      the collar, the eye from a broken.

before she could sip her tea, he said she must have three bites of bread & jam. she took two. he would have her have the third.
stripped to the chemise, a knee at her neck, & a stick from the fire. bloody froth came from her mouth. despite the manner of her death, everyone swears she was never naked. doused thrice with paraffin oil. her answer was not satisfying.

the 'holy morsel' of consecrated bread & cheese— which one was expected to swallow if innocent & choke on if guilty— was a common judicial ordeal until 1215.

milk can put out a fire started by lightning.
the oil burned for half an hour.

Q.
did anyone attempt to extinguish the fire ? did anyone throw water on her ?
A.
my brother William fell into a weakness so my mother threw Easter holy water on him.
Q.
then no one threw water on Bridget ?

hocus-pocus : this is the body.

her first grave was a hollow in a bog. 'scraping the juice of the poor creature off his clothes,' he pressed the body down into the furze with his feet.

despite Michael Cleary's sworn statement that she was dead from a blow to the head, the inquest jury returned a verdict of death by burning.
       the press said 'martyr' : the linguistic path of least resistance— with all the ready-made images of women tied to stakes.
the body would not be pulled flat. in order to fit
Bridget Cleary into her fireplace, her husband used a steel spade. besides, the fireplace was only penultimate. she died on the kitchen floor.

fooles fires, fowles in the firth,
wills with a wisp— a cockerel
decked in colored ribbons let
free on the crags— I've tied
candles to the backs of crabs & set
them loose in churchyards.

Sources

OTHERWISE (AN EKE NAME) SOURCES:

Boym, Svetlana. *The Future of Nostalgia*. Basic Books: New York, 2001.

Cosman, Madeleine Pelner. *Medieval Wordbook*. New York: Checkmark Books, 2001.

Dvorniković, Vladimir. *The Psychology of Yugoslav Melancholy* (1917). qtd. in "Balkan Blues" by Dubravka Ugrešić. *Balkan Blues: Writing out of Yugoslavia*. Ed. Joanna Labon. Illinois: Northwestern U P, 1995.

Howe, Susan. "The Liberties." *The Europe of Trusts*. Los Angeles: Sun & Moon, 1990.

Mathews, Aidan. "The Death of Irish."

Robinson, Tim. *Stones of Aran*. (Volume One: *Pilgrimage*; Volume Two: *Labyrinth*). New York: Penguin, 1989 & 1995.

Rothenberg, Jerome. *Poland/1931*. New York: New Directions, 1974.

Tóibín, Colm & Diarmaid Ferriter, eds. *The Irish Famine: A Documentary*. New York: St. Martin's, 2001.

Williams, William Carlos. "The Descent of Winter." *The Collected Poems of William Carlos Williams*. Vol. I. New York: New Directions, 1991.

ALL ITALICIZED HEADINGS FROM:

Ó Súilleabháin, Seán. *A Handbook of Irish Folklore*. London: Herbert Jenkins, 1963.

ALIBI (THAT IS : ELSEWHERE) SOURCES :

Bishop, Elizabeth. "Questions of Travel." *Elizabeth Bishop: The Complete Poems 1927 - 1979*. New York: Farrar, Straus, & Giroux, 1994.

Cosman, Madeleine Pelner. *Medieval Wordbook*. New York: Checkmark Books, 2001.

de Fréine, Celia. *Faoi Chabáistí is Ríonacha*. Conamara: Cló Iar-Chonnachta, Indreabhán, 2001.

The Malleus Maleficarum

Oppen, George. "Chartres." *New Collected Poems*. New York: New Directions, 2002.

The Oxford English Dictionary

Robinson, Tim. *Stones of Aran*. (Volume One: *Pilgrimage*; Volume Two: *Labyrinth*). New York: Penguin, 1989 & 1995.

Saalman, Howard. *Medieval Cities*. New York: George Braziller, 1968.

Scot, Reginald. *The Discoverie of Witchcraft*. (Great Britain: John Rodker, 1930). New York: Dover, 1972.

Sebald, W.G. *The Rings of Saturn*. New York: New Directions, 1996.

Skelton, John. "Philip Sparrow."

Weiser, Karen. "Forged."

PISEOGS SOURCES :

Benson, E.F. "The Recent 'Witch-Burning' at Clonmel." *The Nineteenth Century*. Vol. 37 (June 1895).

Bourke, Angela. *The Burning of Bridget Cleary*. New York: Viking, 1999.

Briggs, K.M. *The Fairies: In English Literature and Tradition*. Chicago: U Chicago P, 1967.

Grieve, M. *A Modern Herbal*. Harcourt-Brace, 1931. New York: Dover, 1971.

Hoff, Joan & Marian Yeates. *The Cooper's Wife is Missing: The Trials of Bridget Cleary.* New York: Basic Books, 2000.

Jolly, Karen Louise. *Popular Religion in Late Saxon England: Elf Charms in Context.* Chapel Hill: U South Carolina P, 1996.

Ó hEochaidh, Seán, ed. *Síscéalta Ó Thír Chonaill / Fairy Legends from Donegal.* Dublin: Comhairle Bhéaloides Éireann, UCD, 1977.

Ó Súilleabháin, Seán. *A Handbook of Irish Folklore.* London: Herbert Jenkins, 1963.

Thomas, Keith. *Religion and the Decline of Magic.* Oxford: Oxford U P, 1971.

Wilde, Lady Francesca Speranza. *Ancient Legends, Mystic Charms & Superstitions of Ireland.* London: Chatto & Windus, 1925.

With thanks to Celia de Fréine for her Irish-language help.
With thanks to Gregg Biglieri, Barbara Cole, & Kevin Varrone
for their generous readings & advice.

PATTIE MCCARTHY's *bk of (h)rs* was published by Apogee Press in 2002. She received her M.A. in Creative Writing—Poetry from Temple University. She is a founding editor of BeautifulSwimmer Press. Her work has appeared in many magazines and journals, including *26: a journal of poetry & poetics, American Letters & Commentary, ixnay magazine, Kiosk,* and *Pom²*. She has taught literature and writing at Queens College of the City University of New York, Loyola College in Baltimore, and Towson University. She lives in Philadelphia.

Other Titles from Apogee Press

passing world pictures
Valerie Coulton
"Swift and rich, an entire world passes here in vivid glimpses."
—Cole Swensen

Rules of the House
Tsering Wangmo Dhompa
"A lovely explication of 'dharma'—things as they are, and how precious they are."
—Anne Waldman

Discrete Categories Forced into Coupling
Kathleen Fraser
"I love Fraser's extraordinary intelligence, her persistent care for where she is."
—Robert Creeley

Gorgeous Mourning
Alice Jones
"Dazzling poems, wholly taken in by where the words are going."
—Adam Phillips

fine
Stefanie Marlis
"An etymology of our sexual and physical lives, our unknown lives, our daily lives."
— Edward Kleinschmidt Mayes

bk of (h)rs
Pattie McCarthy
"This is simply a gorgeous book."
—Cole Swensen

Speed of Life
Edward Kleinschmidt Mayes
"These are poems at the harsh center of things."
—Eavan Boland

Human Forest
Denise Newman
"Like imbibing a divine elixir, make one realize how thirsty one has been all this time."
—Gillian Conoley

Apprehend
Elizabeth Robinson
"I feel a securing confidence in her poems—as if she had given me her hand."
—Robert Creeley

The Pleasures of C
Edward Smallfield
"These are poems of thrilling uneasiness and probing reward."
—Kathleen Fraser

Oh
Cole Swensen
"Oh is opera cool."
—Marjorie Perloff

dust and conscience
Truong Tran
"Something important is going on, something wonderful."
—Lyn Hejinian

placing the accents
Truong Tran
"A voluptuary of the difficult real. To be entered, and entered. Gratefully."
—Kathleen Fraser

To order, or for more information go to www.apogeepress.com